V
at
Lighthouse Rock

Story by Julie Ellis

Illustrations by Naomi Carolyn Lewis

Emily wanted to be a photographer when she grew up. Collecting photographs was her hobby. She had pictures of all sorts of things.

Emily's brother Jake had a hobby, too. He loved to do magic tricks, and he was always reading science books that explained how to do them.

Emily and Jake and their mother were staying in a camper at Lighthouse Rock for a vacation.

"I really hope I get a camera for my birthday tomorrow," said Emily, one afternoon.

"You know they cost a lot of money," said Jake. "I don't think Mom can afford one."

"Did you see the present Dad sent me?" asked Emily. "It might be a camera."

3

The next morning, Emily opened her birthday presents. Mom had given her some new clothes, Jake had given her a book, and there was some money from Grandma. Emily saved Dad's present until last. Slowly and carefully, she unwrapped it.

Would it be a camera? Emily lifted off the paper. It was only a photograph album. She felt so disappointed.

Jake looked at Emily's presents. "How much money did you get?" he asked. "Maybe you could buy a camera for yourself."

Emily shook her head. It was kind of Grandma to send her money, but cameras were expensive.

5

The next time they went to the supermarket, Emily saw a poster on the bulletin board. The city council was having a photo competition. The photos had to be of the Lighthouse Rock area. The first prize was a camera in a beautiful red case.

Emily was excited. "I'd love to win that camera," she told Jake. She imagined taking photos of people on the beach or a boat on the water.

But she realized that she wouldn't be able to enter the competition, because she didn't have a camera.

Emily wondered if it would be possible to borrow a camera.

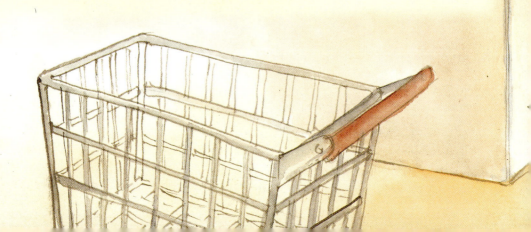

On the way back to the camper, Emily said to Mom, "Do you know anybody who has a camera I could borrow? Then I could enter the photo competition."

Before Mom could answer, Jake asked Emily, "Do you have enough money for one of those cameras that you can use and then throw away?"

Emily smiled. "That's a great idea, Jake," she said. "Why didn't I think of that myself?"

When they got back to the camper, Emily rushed off to count her birthday money and her allowance. She had just enough to buy a throwaway camera.

9

Emily knew that she would have to think carefully about each photo that she took. She couldn't waste any of her film.

That evening, she went down to the beach with Mom and Jake to take a photo of the sunset. There were several other people also photographing the sunset. Emily realized that she would have to take a photo of something different if she were going to have a chance of winning the competition.

Emily decided to photograph the lighthouse. Then she remembered that all the postcards in the bookstore had pictures of the lighthouse on them. It had been photographed on a sunny day, in a storm, and at night.

She had to think of a really clever photo.

The next day, Mom said, "Come for a walk, and stop worrying about that photo competition."

"Okay, Mom," said Emily, and she slipped the camera into her pocket.

On the way, Emily took a photo of a fisherman, and several of children playing in the waves. She only had three pictures left, and she still hadn't taken an exciting, clever photo.

Jake was lying on the grass with one arm outstretched. He shut one eye and looked at his forefinger.

"What are you doing?" asked Emily.

"I'm measuring things," answered Jake. "Did you know that my finger is taller than the lighthouse?"

Emily looked at the lighthouse in the distance. "What do you mean?" she asked.

"Put your arm out straight, Emily," said Jake. "From this distance, you can hold the lighthouse between your finger and your thumb. I read about it in one of my science books. It's called an optical illusion. I can even hold it in the palm of my hand!"

"Jake, that's it!" said Emily. "An optical illusion." She made Jake stand with one arm outstretched. Then she moved back until it looked as though the lighthouse were sitting on the palm of Jake's hand.

"I've got it. An original photo! I'm going to win this competition," said Emily.

On the day that the competition results were published, Emily and Jake rushed to the newsstand early, to buy the local newspaper.

Emily felt hopeful and excited. The winning photo was published on the front page. But it wasn't her photo. It was a photo of the cliffs and the sea.

She hadn't won. Emily felt tears pricking in her eyes. She handed the paper to Jake and ran down to the beach.

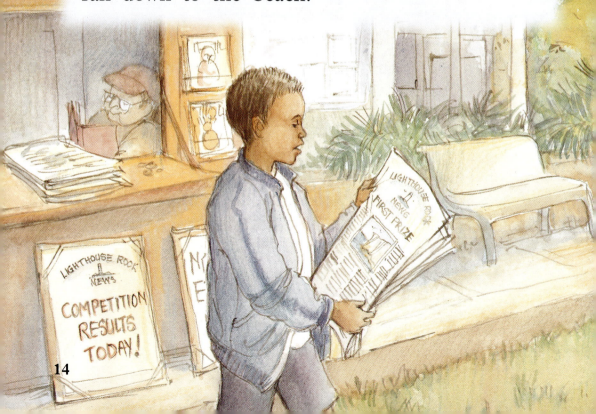

When she returned to the camper, Emily was annoyed to see Jake and Mom smiling cheerfully.

"Look, Emily," said Jake, holding the paper out to her. "Your photo's on page three! You didn't read all of the results."

"The judges thought your photo was so good that they have awarded you a special *Young Photographer* prize," said Mom. "It's a camera!"

"I can hardly believe it!" laughed Emily. "I'm famous! And now I'll have a proper camera at last."